snapshot·picture·library

SHARKS

snapshot•picture•library

SHARKS

FOG CITY PRESS

Published by Fog City Press,
a division of Weldon Owen Inc.
415 Jackson Street
San Francisco, CA 94111 USA
www.weldonowen.com

WELDON OWEN INC.
Group Publisher, Bonnier Publishing Group John Owen
President, CEO Terry Newell
Senior VP, International Sales Stuart Laurence
VP, Sales and New Business Development Amy Kaneko
VP, Publisher Roger Shaw
Executive Editor Elizabeth Dougherty
Editorial Assistant Katharine Moore
Associate Creative Director Kelly Booth
Senior Designer William Mack
Designer Michel Gadwa
Production Director Chris Hemesath
Production Manager Michelle Duggan
Color Manager Teri Bell

A WELDON OWEN PRODUCTION
© 2010 Weldon Owen Inc.

Library of Congress Control Number: 2009938074

ISBN 978 1 74089 957 4

10 9 8 7 6 5 4 3 2 1
2010 2011 2012 2013

Printed by Tien Wah Press in Singapore.

Sharks are amazing creatures.
Most sharks are fierce fish
that hunt other sea creatures.
They have very sharp teeth for
biting food. But you should
not be afraid of them. As long
as you keep out of their way,
sharks will leave you alone.

Sharks live in oceans all over the
world. But many people have
never seen one. Much of the
time, sharks are far out to sea and
deep underwater. Sharks can be
many beautiful shapes and sizes.
Which one is your favorite?

A shark has long, pointed fins that stick out of its body. The fin on its back can sometimes poke out of the water.

Sharks swim by beating their
tails from side to side. The
side fins help them to steer.

Large sharks
can swim as fast
as a powerboat.
They can jump
out of the water
when hunting
creatures near
the surface.

Sharks breathe underwater by passing water over feathery structures inside their heads called gills.

Most sharks are
fast hunters. They
eat animals such
as fish, dolphins,
squid, and seals.

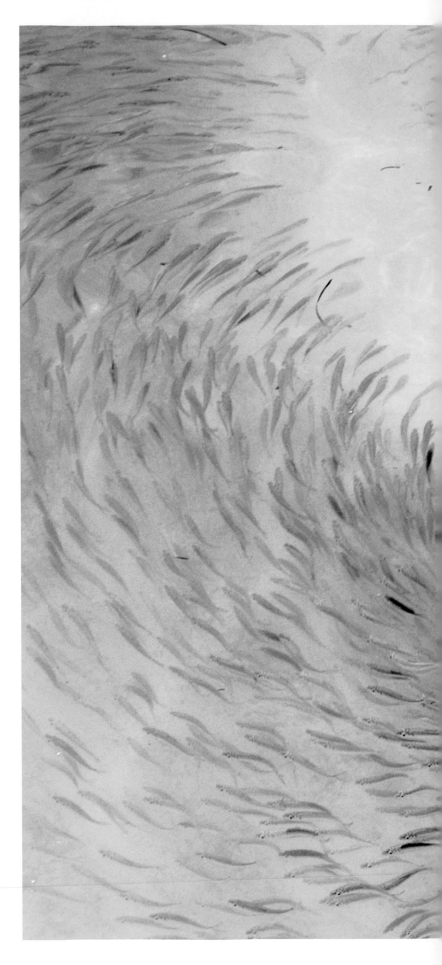

A shark's skin can sense electricity
coming from the bodies of other
animals. This helps sharks find food.

Many sharks have eyes that point up and forward. They cannot see much of what is happening beneath them.

Sharks have wide mouths full of
pointed teeth lined up in two or
three rows, so every bite counts!

Sharks wait for the right time to attack before ambushing their prey. Then they take a giant bite.

Smelling food makes sharks very hungry. When a group of sharks find some food, they rush after it. This is called a feeding frenzy.

The most powerful hunter is the great white shark. It grows thousands of teeth during its life.

The whale shark
is the biggest fish
of all. It is as long
as a bus, but it is a
gentle giant. The
whale shark eats
tiny bits of food
called plankton
by filtering them
through its gills.

The sharks on this page grow to be about 5 feet (1.5 meters) long. The zebra shark opposite grows to be twice as long.

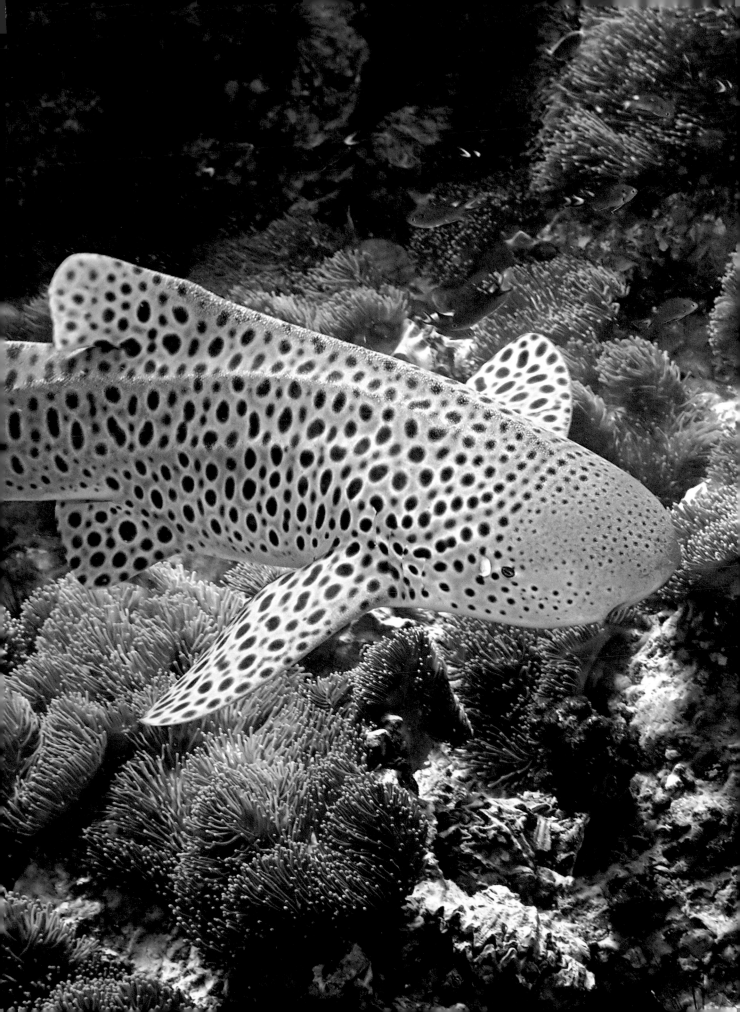

Hammerhead sharks look strange! Their wide heads help them swim and sniff out prey.

Some sharks
look for food
on the seabed.
They use their
fleshy whiskers,
called barbels,
to find food
in the sand.

Coral reefs are home to a lot of sharks. Other animals hide from them.

Sharks search for food everywhere. These sharks are exploring a shipwreck.

Sharks do not need bright light to find food. They often hunt at night or in deep, dark water.

Big sharks live in deep water.
Their skin colors can make
them hard to see in the water.

Sharks that
live in shallow
water often
have patterned
skin to blend
in with their
surroundings.

Some small fish, such as remora, follow sharks around. These fish nibble on the sharks' skin, cleaning it and eating any leftovers.

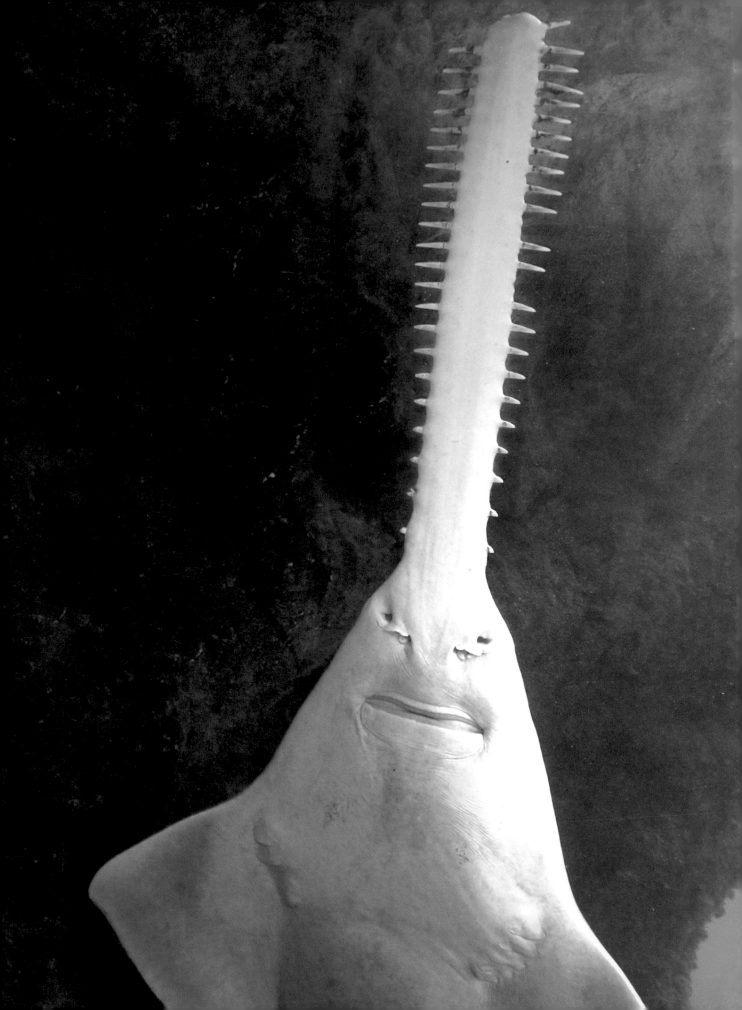

Sharks have some strange relatives. The sawfish has teeth pointing sideways! Rays are as flat as pancakes.

Many baby sharks hatch from egg cases like these. An egg case is called a mermaid's purse.

Expert divers can get very
close to sharks to study them.

Divers watch the most dangerous sharks from inside a safety cage.

Sometimes
sharks appear in
scary movies.

A good place
to see a real
shark is at an
aquarium, which
is a kind of
underwater
zoo. Have you
seen a shark?

Great white shark

The largest hunting shark in the world grows to 20 feet (6 m) long. Most of the animal is gray. Only its belly is actually white.

Whale shark

The largest shark grows to 40 feet (12 m) and is also the biggest type of fish living today. It feeds all the time, filtering tiny bits of food called plankton from the water.

Sand tiger shark

This brown-skinned shark hunts near coasts in most parts of the world. Sand tigers even team up to trap groups of fish. The shark's teeth are very pointed and crooked.

Blacktip reef shark

A common small shark around reefs, the blacktip gets its name from the dark markings on many of its fins. Blacktips grow to 6.5 feet (2 m) long.

Spotted wobbegong

This odd-looking shark lives in shallow waters around the coast of Australia. Its spotty pattern helps it stay hidden on the seabed.

Epaulette shark

This little shark lives on the coral reefs in Australia and New Guinea. It crawls around the seabed looking for worms and shrimp.